Cities through Time

Daily Life in Ancient and Modern

by Steve Cory

illustrations by Ray Webb

RP

Runestone Press/Minneapolis
A Division of the Lerner Publishing Group

The *Cities through Time* series is produced by Runestone Press, a division of the Lerner Publishing Group, in cooperation with Greenleaf Publishing, Inc., Geneva, Illinois.

Cover design by Michael Tacheny
Text design by Melanie Lawson

The Lerner Publishing Group
241 First Avenue North
Minneapolis, Minnesota 55401

Website address: www.lernerbooks.com

Library of Congress Cataloging-in-Publication Data

Cory, Steve.
Daily life in ancient and modern Mexico City / by Steve Cory ; illustrations by Ray Webb.
p. cm. — (Cities through time)
Includes index.
Summary: A historical exploration of events and daily life in Mexico City in both ancient and modern times.
ISBN 0-8225-3212-3 (lib. bdg. : alk. paper)
1. Mexico City (Mexico)—History—Juvenile literature. 2. Mexico City (Mexico)—Social life and customs—Juvenile literature. 4. Mexico City (Mexico)—Social conditions—Juvenile literature. [1. Mexico City (Mexico)] I. Webb, Ray, ill. II. Title. III. Series.
F1386.C678 1999
972'.53—dc21 98-18312

Manufactured in the United States of America
1 2 3 4 5 6 - JR - 04 03 02 01 00 99

Contents

The altitude of the valley varies from 6,800 to 7,900 feet above sea level.
The early residents hunted mammoths in the Valley of Mexico.
A high water table in the valley continues to affect Mexico City.
Game, plentiful fishing, and pleasant weather attracted nomadic hunters and gatherers.

Introduction

Mexico City, or Ciudad de México in Spanish, arose in a place whose natural features have given its inhabitants problems and benefits for centuries. Although the city is at an elevation of 7,350, it also sits at the bottom of a great basin called the Valley of Mexico that is surrounded by high mountains. The bowl-shaped valley traps smog, making pollution one of Mexico City's biggest problems. Modern Mexico City sits on the bed of what was once Lake Texcoco, and the land remains spongy and prone to flooding. The Valley of Mexico also lies on a major fault line, creating the possibility for damaging earthquakes.

Despite these problems, the city's location has many advantages. It has a wonderful climate. Heavy rains often fall from June to September, but temperatures are almost never cold enough to require a jacket. And because of its high elevation, Mexico City escapes the intense heat that engulfs the rest of Mexico much of the time. For its ancient inhabitants—including the Aztecs—the Valley of Mexico became a rich source of food, producing enough to support a large population. As a result, highly advanced cultures developed. They used complex technologies and had well-ordered social systems. Because of its height, Mexico City was difficult to attack and became an ideal location for the capital of the great Aztec Empire. Later the site became the capital of the United Mexican States, as the Mexican nation is officially called.

For much of its history, Mexico City has been a seat of power. Aztecs, Spaniards, and independent Mexicans all ruled from here. The location lacked navigable rivers, and beasts of burden were rare because hay and feed were hard to come by. For these reasons, early cultures depended on manual labor, including slaves. Poor people in outlying areas became the workforce and came to resent the rulers of Mexico City.

Modern Mexicans are proud of their capital. Although Mexico City covers less than 1 percent of Mexico, it holds almost 20 percent of the country's population and is among the most populous cities in the world. People flock to it in great numbers every day, both to visit and to live. The city's impressive central square, called the Zócalo, dates to Aztec times. The streets of the poorest sections are filled with color, music, and laughter as street vendors, entertainers, and hardworking people jostle in an atmosphere full of life.

The City Called Teotihuacán

Beginning in the first century A.D., about 25 miles north of present-day Mexico City, a great city named Teotihuacán came into being. Its people learned to farm the land, constructing terraces in the hillsides to catch and hold rainwater and using water from underground springs for annual irrigation. They discovered maize (corn), a valuable food that could keep throughout the year.

In Teotihuacán workers laid out the streets in a grid pattern and lined them with stone and brick houses. Merchants, farmers, warriors, and craftspeople inhabited their own districts. Temples and palaces dominated the central district where rulers and priests lived in splendor.

The grid pattern of Teotihuacán would be repeated by the Aztecs when they founded Tenochtitlán, the future Mexico City.

Large religious processions watched by many thousands of people filled a wide main street. Artisans decorated great stone buildings with intricate carvings. The people of Teotihuacán made concrete for their floors and plastered the outside of their buildings. They built a canal to bring water to the city.

The Great Goddess was the most important god, especially at the beginning of the Teotihuacán culture. She is always shown with her face covered, usually giving water, seeds, and other good things to her worshipers. She held the promise of good harvests, which the people needed to survive.

Over time Teotihuacán developed into a great military power. Its rulers became used to vast wealth, although most farmers and other workers lived in poverty. Modern archaeologists think that Teotihuacán declined largely because of a revolt by the people, who were fed up with their oppressive rulers.

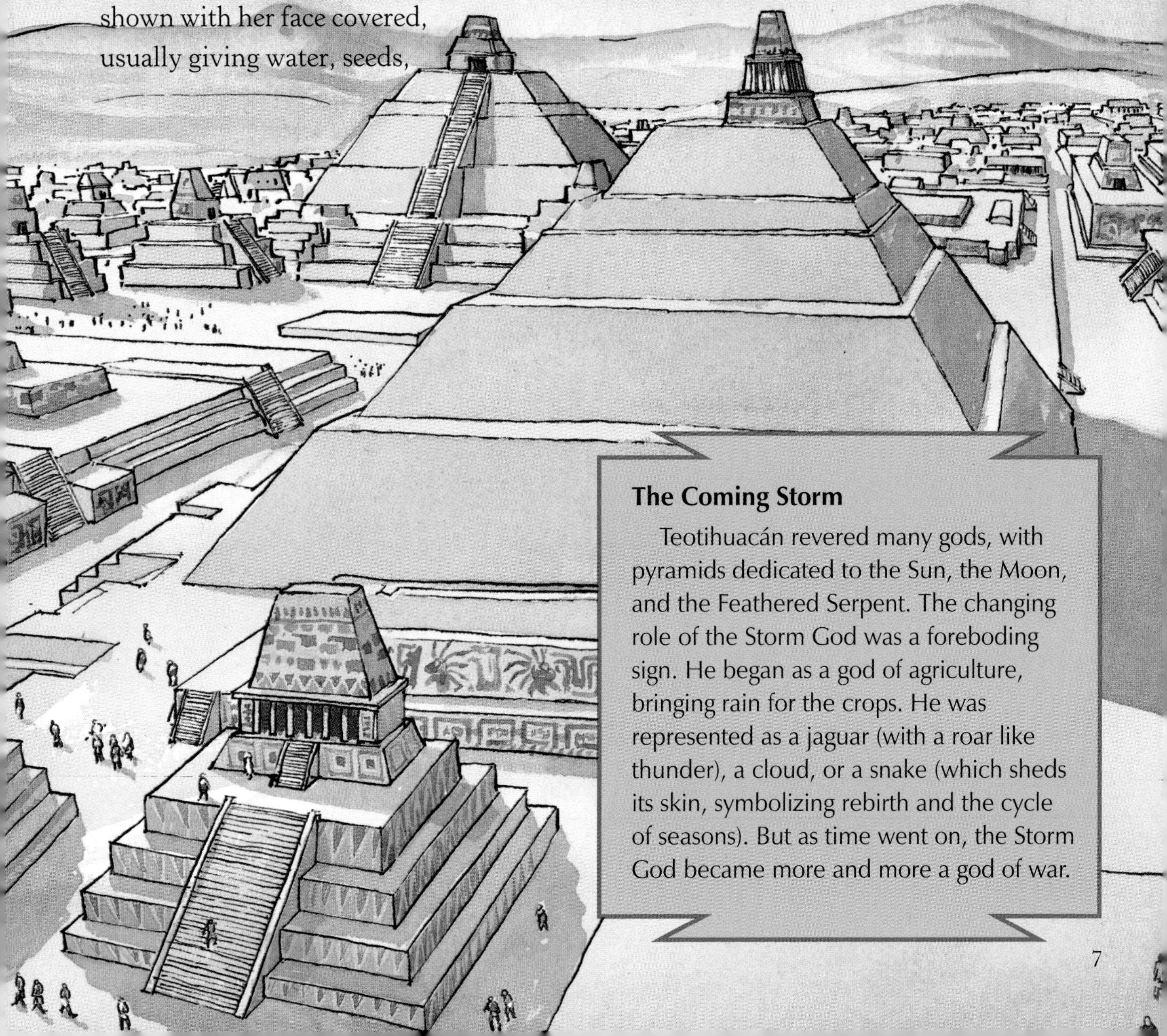

The Coming Storm

Teotihuacán revered many gods, with pyramids dedicated to the Sun, the Moon, and the Feathered Serpent. The changing role of the Storm God was a foreboding sign. He began as a god of agriculture, bringing rain for the crops. He was represented as a jaguar (with a roar like thunder), a cloud, or a snake (which sheds its skin, symbolizing rebirth and the cycle of seasons). But as time went on, the Storm God became more and more a god of war.

Floating Farms

Throughout the ancient world, irrigation gave people a stable food supply and allowed their cultures to flourish. The residents of the Valley of Mexico also built irrigation systems, but they added a unique twist. Because they were in a valley with lakes at the bottom, it was difficult to bring lake water to higher land. So they did the reverse—they brought land to the water. They created islands, called *chinampas,* and then planted them with various crops that yielded several harvests per year.

To create a chinampa, workers made a raft out of branches or reeds. Then they dredged mud from the lake and piled it on the reeds. The resulting soil was rich, and wood and bone farm tools could easily work it. To speed production, seeds wére planted on the mainland. After they sprouted, they were transplanted to the chinampas, where they grew quickly.

Planting and harvesting the same crops in the same field tends to deplete the soil's nitrogen—a key element to help crops grow. Teotihuacán farmers in the Valley of Mexico learned to intercrop—that is, to put different crops in the same field. Plants such as beans and squash shared space with maize. These smaller plants fertilized the soil by giving nitrogen back so farming could continue for many years.

The diet of the valley's peoples took advantage of these flourishing crops. They ground maize into flour. Beans, squash, and chilies were common. Small fish and other animals provided protein. For nutritious greens, they had *tecuilatl,* an algae pressed into cakes.

Floating beds, called chinampas, allowed early farmers to plant on lakes using wood and bone implements.

Aztecs Arrive

According to legend, the Aztecs wandered for centuries in the wilderness until they came to the Valley of Mexico. Huitzilopochtli, the Hummingbird God, told them to look for a lake with a small island. They would know it was the right place when they saw an eagle perched on a cactus eating a snake. The Aztecs saw this very scene in the Valley of Mexico and stopped wandering. In time, they built their capital city of Tenochtitlán on the site. The modern Mexican flag has a picture of an eagle clutching a snake, commemorating the birth of the nation's greatest city.

That's the legend. In fact, the Aztecs arrived in the Valley of Mexico in the middle of the thirteenth century, when several warring peoples were fighting one another. The Aztecs were conquered and enslaved by the Culhuacán, who used the Aztecs as mercenaries—warriors for hire. The slaves then conquered the masters and came to control most of the valley. Most of their gods, including Huitzilopochtli, actually originated in the Valley of Mexico.

Aztec society was at first organized into small family clans called *calpulli,* each of which had its own laws and rulers. Members of the calpulli were treated more or less as equals. But as the rulers got more powerful, the common people became more like slaves than citizens.

The Aztec marketplace *(detail)* as painted by the modern Mexican artist Diego Rivera

Lake Texcoco
Temple to
Huitzilopochtli

Magnificent Tenochtitlán

By the sixteenth century, Tenochtitlán had a population of perhaps 300,000—a huge number of people at that time. And on the outskirts of the city lived another 400,000. Urban and suburban Tenochtitlán appeared to be one huge metropolitan area joined together with a system of roads and canals.

It was an island city, surrounded by Lake Texcoco. The massive 10-mile dike of Nezahualcóyotl was an engineering marvel. It not only protected the city from flood but also allowed the chinampas to be farmed near the city. The homes of the rich were sparkling white with lime plaster and had banners made of bright-colored feathers flying atop towers. At the center of the city was a large area devoted to religious observances. Its most impressive structure was the pyramid-shaped temple to Huitzilopochtli. Rebuilt several times on the same spot, the temple honored the place where, according to legend, the Aztecs had seen the eagle sitting on the cactus clutching the snake. Temples to other gods, sumptuous residences for Aztec priests, and a huge marketplace were located in the central district. Here also was the king's palace, with its treasury filled with vast wealth. Signs of violence existed, too. A gigantic rack, called the *tzompantli*, displayed the skulls of thousands of people sacrificed to the gods. The steps of Huitzilopochtli's temple were spattered with blood.

The chinampas helped establish Tenochtitlán but could not come close to providing so many people with food, let alone riches. Tenochtitlán was rich because it was the center of a great empire covering much of modern-day Mexico. The payments made by conquered peoples kept food, riches, and slaves pouring into the city for centuries.

Aztec Warriors

There is nothing like death in war
Nothing like the flowery death
So precious to Him who gives life
Far off I see it: my heart yearns for it!
—Aztec poem

Hated and feared by their neighbors, the Aztecs did have a sense of fair play when it came to warfare. If a town that they were about to attack did not have enough weapons to defend itself, the Aztecs would give the people weapons so that the battle would be a true test of the warriors skill and bravery.

Houses, Streets, Canals

If you were a middle-class resident of Tenochtitlán, you probably would have made your home in a multistoried building created of plain mud brick. Most families had only one or two rooms with few windows. The floor was hardened earth. A simple mat bed was one of the few pieces of furniture, because only the wealthy had chairs, tables, and storage chests. Most of the cooking took place in patio areas outdoors. Surrounding the apartment building were small plots of land where residents could plant vegetable and flower gardens.

Each neighborhood was named after an Aztec subgroup and had its own marketplace and religious centers. Boys received military training at a neighborhood school, and local judges handled disputes. Tenochtitlán was extremely clean. Apart from times of flooding, the streets were well drained. Garbage was collected regularly and hauled away on barges. A crew of more than a thousand men swept and washed the streets every day. The people bathed often.

Nearly every street had a stone-edged canal running alongside it, and most everyone owned a canoe. Barges and canoes that plied the city's canals allowed goods to move throughout the city quickly and efficiently.

Lake Texcoco's water was still too salty for people to drink. To supply hundreds of thousands of people with fresh water, the Aztecs built an impressive aqueduct. Two separate stone and wood channels, each six feet wide, carried water from an underground spring three miles away. Only one channel was used at a time. The second was a backup, in case of damage to the first. Rich people had water piped directly to their homes. For common people, water was carried in large jugs on canoes.

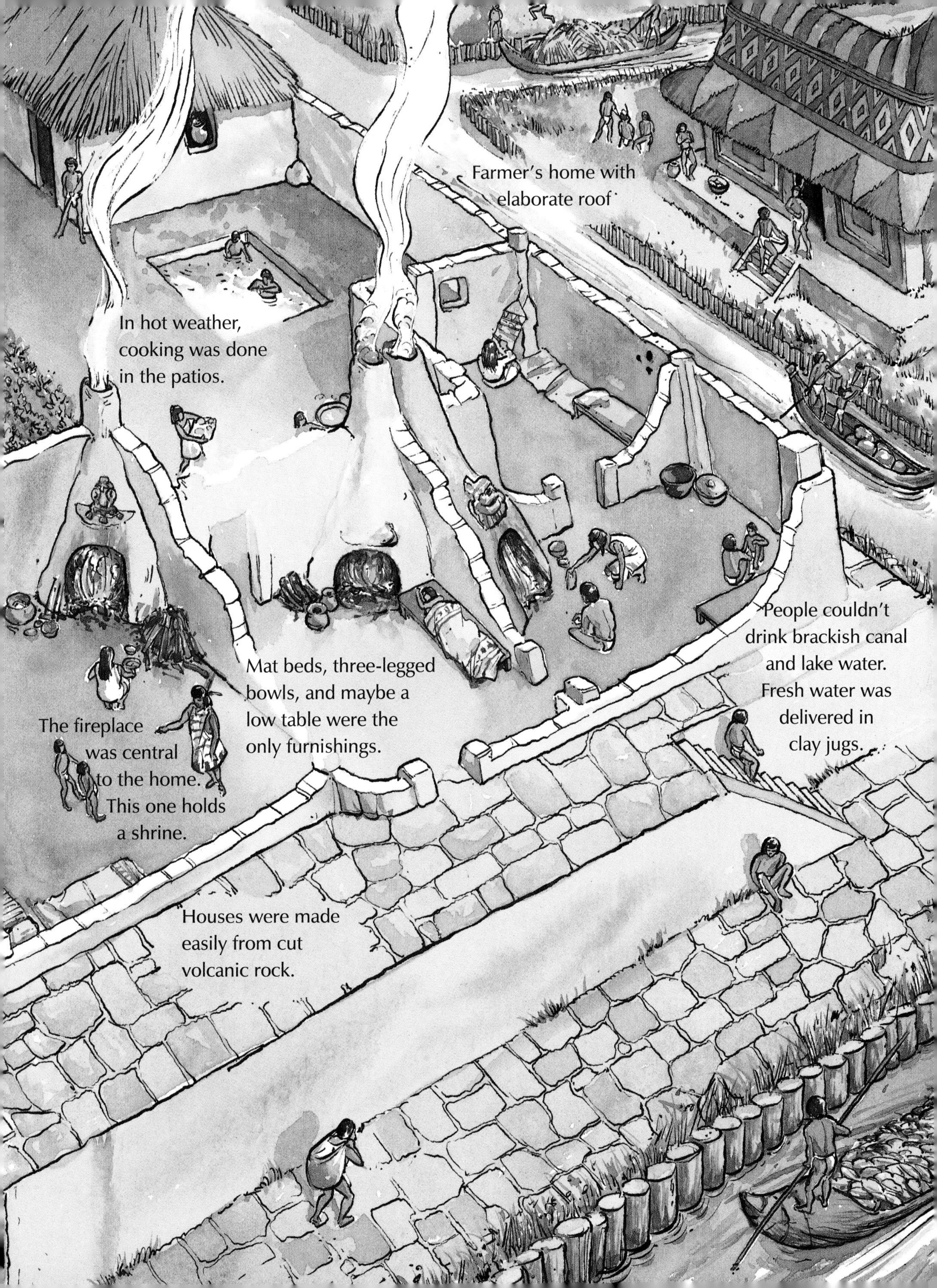

Farmer's home with elaborate roof
In hot weather, cooking was done in the patios.
Mat beds, three-legged bowls, and maybe a low table were the only furnishings.
People couldn't drink brackish canal and lake water. Fresh water was delivered in clay jugs.
The fireplace was central to the home. This one holds a shrine.
Houses were made easily from cut volcanic rock.

Marketplaces

Just about everything that was made or grown throughout the vast Aztec Empire could be found at the marketplaces of Tenochtitlán. The spot rang with the sounds of birds of all kinds, including hawks and eagles. Food animals such as rabbits, dogs, deer, fish, turtles, and frogs were on sale. Vendors hawked jewelry made of feathers, copper, silver, and gold. Foodstalls offered maize, beans, tomatoes, onions, artichokes, and fruit. Other goods included construction materials such as lime and lumber and all sorts of materials for clothing.

The central district held the city's largest marketplace. Every day as many as 60,000 people crowded into it to

buy and sell food, clothing, and works of art. Although it was crowded, the market was surprisingly orderly. The Aztecs did not have money but used standard items for exchange—cacao beans, copper, precious stones, gold dust, and pieces of clothing were common. There were no scales for weighing things. Instead, everything was either counted or measured for size. If there was an argument, it was settled immediately, either in nearby courthouses set up for the purpose or by government regulators paid to walk through the market and resolve disputes.

Gathering on the fringes of the marketplace were groups of Aztec gamblers. Games like *patolli,* played on a board with marked beans that were used like dice, became a passion. Some men were reported to have gambled away their houses and even their wives and children.

Sacrifices

Religion was a vital part of Aztec life, and religious rites took place frequently. Most of the rituals revolved around the farming cycle. According to the Aztec religion, the gods, especially Huitzilopochtli, gave good things to the people who offered the best sacrifices. Good harvests and victory in war, for example, depended on having the gods on your side.

The Aztecs believed that Huitzilopochtli and the other gods got strength from offerings of blood. Priests often sliced their own earlobes and tongues and presented the blood to Huitzilopochtli. The common people cut their ears and offered the blood in some ceremonies. The king himself was expected to give some of his own blood to the rites.

Of all the blood offerings, the people believed that the heart of a sacrificial victim held the most power. Priests slashed open the person's chest and tore out the heart while it was still beating. Blood from the heart was sprinkled on Huitzilopochtli's altar.

Some victims thought sacrifice was an honor. Warriors who died in battle, women who died in childbirth, and people who were killed as sacrifices were thought to have earned a privileged place in the afterlife. Captured soldiers often chose to be sacrificed rather than be enslaved to attain religious merit and to avoid the shame of defeat.

As an Aztec official looks on, prisoners of war were sacrificed to the Sun God.

Multibladed knife used in sacrifices

During famines or when the Aztecs worried about the future of their kingdom, thousands were offered as sacrifice.

It is not true that we come on this earth to live. We come only to sleep, only to dream.
—Aztec poem

To gain favor with Tlaloc, the god of rain, children were often sacrificed. In some ceremonies, victims died a slow death. In one rite, Aztec warriors wore the flayed skin of men they had captured in war. Sometimes the kings of conquered peoples were made to watch as their own soldiers were sacrificed. The Aztecs practiced human sacrifice on such a large scale that they incited the hatred and shock of their neighbors.

Motecuhzoma: King and God

Aztec kings lived in great splendor, wielded vast military power, and amassed great wealth. But Motecuhzoma, or Montezuma *(right),* the last Aztec king, outdid them all. After coming to the throne, he executed or exiled local leaders and generals. He enslaved the sons of lords and princes. He also did something no other Aztec ruler had done before—Motecuhzoma declared himself to be a god. Whenever he walked by, everyone fell on their faces until he'd passed.

There were good reasons why he wanted the people to fear him. Although the Aztec realm was large and wealthy, it was in trouble. Enemy states were growing more powerful, and conquered peoples were becoming more rebellious. The population was increasing, making it hard to feed everyone. Farmers were forced to toil ceaselessly to produce the largest possible harvests. Motecuhzoma believed that ruthlessness was the only way to keep the empire from falling apart. To control the population, he ordered more human sacrifices to be performed and embarked on a series of military campaigns, even against people who once had been allies of the Aztecs.

Motecuhzoma lived a life of almost unimaginable power and grandeur. A small army of musicians, jesters, dancers, and acrobats entertained him. Although a light eater, he was presented with more than 100 different dishes to choose from every day. He had more than a thousand wives. His zoo included an aviary with hundreds of species of birds. Ten large rooms held salt- and freshwater pools filled with many varieties of fish. Jaguars, pumas, foxes, and hundreds of other land animals kept a staff of 200 veterinarians busy.

For all his power, Motecuhzoma was nervous. He often consulted the stars, and he became afraid at what he saw as evil portents. Thunderless lightning had damaged a temple; a strange comet seemed to bleed fire; a whirlpool appeared in Lake Texcoco and flooded part of the city. These and other omens seemed to fulfill prophecies that foretold the downfall of the Aztec Empire. Worst of all, a messenger brought paintings depicting strange bearded men with white skin who had arrived in huge boats and were heading toward the capital city.

Quetzalcoatl and the Spaniards

Long before the Aztecs came to power, various groups in the Valley of Mexico had worshiped Quetzalcoatl, a god who took the form of a serpent with a feathered head. Quetzalcoatl hated human sacrifice, asking instead for offerings of butterflies, birds, or snakes. Ancient legends said that although other gods had defeated Quetzalcoatl, he promised some day to regain his rule over Mexico.

Over time people came to detest the Aztecs and their cruel rule, and devotion to Quetzalcoatl grew. The enemies, allies, and even subjects of the Aztec Empire became worshipers. Prophets said Quetzalcoatl would come back to destroy the Aztec kingdom.

Hernán Cortés and his small army of Spaniards landed in Mexico in 1519, the very year when a prophecy predicted the return of Quetzalcoatl. The Europeans had arrived from beyond the horizon of the sea, where only the gods could dwell.

When we saw all those cities and villages built in the water, and the other great towns on dry land, and that straight and level causeway leading to Mexico, we were astounded. These great towns and pyramids and buildings rising from the water, all made of stone, seemed like an enchanted vision.... Some of our soldiers asked whether it was not all a dream.

—Spanish visitor,
Bernal Díaz del Castillo

A Spanish soldier on horseback looked like a single, fearsome creature. Spanish guns and cannons made unheard-of noise and did shocking damage. The soldiers' armor, white faces, and beards were strange.

At first Motecuhzoma treated Cortés and his men like gods. It soon became clear, however, that these men were intent on conquest. The Spaniards were forced to flee the city, barely escaping with their lives. Yet within two years after landing in Mexico, this small army was able to overthrow one of the most powerful empires in the world.

One reason the Spaniards were successful was because they fought by different rules. For the Aztecs, battle was a sacred duty and should take place between evenly matched warriors. They feared the Spaniards, but they also saw them as cowards, because they used superior weapons and shot at people from a safe distance.

Most important, the Spaniards conquered with the help of many thousands of local groups who had become fed up with Aztec rule. People flocked to the Spaniards, eager to help with the destruction of the Aztec Empire.

A watercolor by a European sailor shows an Aztec lookout in a tree warning of the arrival of a Spanish ship.

A Colonial City

Much of Tenochtitlán was destroyed during the war between the Spaniards and the Aztecs, a conflict that came to be called the Spanish Conquest, or La Conquista. After their victory, the Spaniards decided to keep the site as the capital of their new colonial empire. They repaired the damage of their siege and renamed the city Mexico City after Mexica, one of the names the Aztecs called themselves.

Tenochtitlán had been an ideal capital for the great Aztec Empire. The Spaniards realized that Mexico City could work well for them, too. The tribute payments that had flowed into the hands of the Aztecs could go into Spanish coffers. Aztec-controlled silver mines could produce riches for the conquerors. And the local people could be an unpaid labor force.

Although the city took on a Spanish look, the basic plan of the city remained the same. The grid of streets and canals and the flat-roofed apartment buildings with gardens and patios survived. Neighborhoods, organized around governmental and religious buildings, were left largely intact.

Early Spanish buildings were built like fortresses, with thick walls and doors, with narrow windows, and even with drawbridges. But the Spaniards soon found out that they need not fear the local people, whom they called Indians. Their religion had been destroyed, and many had been killed by diseases the Europeans had unknowingly introduced. The Spaniards forced the Indians to rebuild the city. Workers carried backbreaking loads for miles. Many were killed, either crushed by beams falling from great heights or simply worked to death.

Spanish sources of the time suggest that the Indians took pride in the project and worked enthusiastically. One visitor even said they sang and shouted, "with voices that never ceased night and day, for such was the great fervor with which they erected the city in those early years."

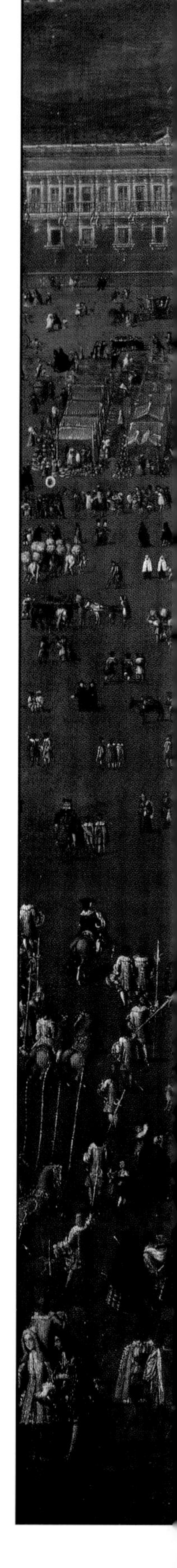

By the 1600s, European carriages and strutting gentry were filling the main plaza of Mexico City.

Indians and Priests

European missionaries saw that the Indians had much in common with Roman Catholicism, including ornate places of worship, liturgy, a religious calendar, and a priesthood. Yet Indian, and especially Aztec, religion was based on human sacrifice. Some saw the Indians as only misguided, while others viewed them as possessed by the devil. Some Spanish clerics believed the epidemics that had led to mass death were the price Aztecs paid for human sacrifice. The pope (the Roman Catholic leader) scolded the clerics for this attitude, asserting that Indians were human beings capable of understanding. They should be converted to the faith.

Nowhere else was the Catholic Church so successful in winning converts as it was in Mexico. Many Indians, completely demoralized and disillusioned with their old religion, helped the Spaniards tear down temples. Often the Catholic Church came to the aid of the Indians. It provided low-rent housing and ran hospitals and schools for the very poor. At one point, when thousands of Indians were starving because landowners were hoarding food, church officials threatened the landowners with eternal damnation if they did not release food to the Indians.

Some Indians maintained their old religion, hiding statues in the walls—sometimes even behind Christian altars—and gathering at night for secret ceremonies. Yet within 50 years of the conquest, most Indians had converted to Christianity. Some blended it with ideas from their old religion, including the view that Jesus and the saints, like the Indians, had endured great suffering. Bloody images of Jesus on the cross also suggest this theme. Similar to Aztec temples, the churches in Mexico City were often ornate, with gold decorations and intricate statues of Mary, Jesus, saints, and angels.

It was common for Indians to see miraculous appearances of Jesus or the Virgin Mary at places where shrines to Aztec gods had once stood. The cult of the Virgin of Guadalupe, where pilgrims still flock by the thousands, began when an Indian saw a vision of a dark-skinned Mary on the former site of a temple to Tonantzin, the mother of Aztec gods.

The Tumult of 1692

The Indians had no immunity against European diseases, especially smallpox. People died in great numbers. Before the Spaniards arrived, Mexico held 12 to 25 million Indians. By the early 1600s, only 1.2 million remained. The survivors led lives of misery. Many Spaniards considered the Indians less than human and treated them like animals. Forced labor was common. As the Indian population dwindled, slaves from the African continent were brought in.

In Mexico City, the Indians, who made up the great majority of the population, lived in small buildings of clay, wood, and cornstalks amid the tall buildings of the Spaniards. Laws forbade the Indians from speaking their own languages, practicing their ancient religion, and owning land.

A complicated social system, based on ancestry and skin color, developed during the seventeenth century. A child with one European (white) parent and one Indian parent was called a mestizo. A mulatto came from the intermarriage of a black person and white person. The child of a black person and an Indian was a zambo. If one parent was white and one a mulatto, then the child was known as a

morisco and so on. A person's ethnic background determined privileges. The more European-looking one's color and features were, the greater the opportunities one had.

The poor people of Mexico did not always accept this fate. One of the times when they rose up has been called the Tumult of 1692. In the summer of 1691, a flood filled all the roads of the city, making it difficult to transport food and other supplies. In the countryside, crops were destroyed. An eclipse of the sun convinced many that evil times were coming. By 1692 the city was in the grip of famine.

In June of 1692, the poorer sections of the city erupted in violence. They joined together, with the people shouting, "Down with the Spaniards who are eating our corn!" Church officials tried to calm the mob but to no avail. The crowd broke into palaces, stores, and municipal buildings, looting and setting many buildings on fire.

As a result of the uprising, the Spanish community became fearful and grew more tightly knit. Strict social and geographical boundaries were put in place. The Indians, for example, had to stay in their own neighborhoods, apart from black people or people of mixed heritages. Spanish officials thought that when the multiracial majority got together, they were likely to become violent.

On the north side of the plaza was the enormous and ornate Metropolitan Cathedral *(below)*. To the east, the National Palace housed the presidency and the Mexican legislature. On the west side lay the Monte de Piedad, a huge pawn shop run by the government. Other buildings included the mint, the courts, and a jail.

The Zócalo

In the early 1800s, Mexico was engaged in a long fight for independence from Spain. Most of the fighting took place in the countryside, away from the city. In Mexico City, most people, even the very poor, remained loyal to the colonial government. But as refugees poured in, services were cut because of lack of money. Garbage was not removed, packs of wild dogs roamed free, and uncontrolled flooding spread deadly diseases.

In 1821 Agustín de Iturbide put together an effective democratic movement that gained Mexico its independence from Spain. Roman Catholicism would be the official religion of the new country. The strict social system and slavery were officially abolished. Soon, however, it became clear that Iturbide did not want Mexico to be a democracy, and he took on the title of emperor of Mexico. In spite of the official laws, independent Mexico was little different from colonial Mexico. European ancestry was still necessary for success.

Mexico City remained the economic and political hub of Mexico. And the main plaza—the same focal point used by the Aztecs and the Spaniards—remained the center of the city. In the 1820s, a large statue of the Spanish king Charles IV was removed, leaving behind an empty pedestal, or *zócalo* in Spanish, giving the plaza its nickname.

And just as in Aztec and Spanish times, the marketplace was filled every day with more than 30 types of merchants, each with their own musical cry. Charcoal sellers, bakers of small cakes, fruit vendors, and many others had to juggle their goods, using their heads as well as their hands, as they sang their jingles. *Cabeceros*, with their portable restaurants, worked in pairs. One carried the meat, the other a small oven. *Aguadors* lugged water from public fountains to the neighborhoods in large earthen jugs.

Mexico City's main plaza in the 1800s

A City of Great Wealth

For centuries nearly all the wealth produced in Mexico flowed into Mexico City, mainly into the hands of Mexicans of Spanish descent. In time wealthy Mexicans also became involved in overseas trade. Many of the rich in Mexico City owned haciendas, large agricultural estates worked by an unpaid labor force of Indians and people of mixed race. Many hacienda owners rarely visited their farmlands.

In the early nineteenth century, Alameda Park,west of the Zócalo, was the place to be seen. Poorer classes were kept out. Horse-drawn carriages were ornamented with silver, gold, and jewels. In the park, women never left their carriages, and men stayed on horseback. Clothing was also designed to impress. The wealthy wore expensive silks, even sporting hatbands made of diamonds or pearls.

The largest mansions cost up to 300,000 pesos, in a city where 300 pesos per year was considered a good salary. On the outside, palaces were often covered with expensive tile or granite. Thick, richly decorated doors featured coats of arms. Inner patios often contained fountains and large statues. The rich ate on imported porcelain with fine silverware and crystal glassware. Even small children wore gaudy jewelry as part of their everyday dress. A family with less than two servants per family member was considered to be doing poorly.

A panorama of Mexico City

Of every one hundred people you come across, only one is fully clothed and wears shoes. In this city, one sees two diametrically opposed extremes: great wealth and maximum poverty.
—Father Francisco de Ajofrin

Houses of the Poor

In the first half of the nineteenth century, Mexico was ruled by a series of corrupt military leaders who plunged the country into anarchy. Mexico and Mexico City grew poorer. Earthquakes and fires destroyed many homes. The elite classes grew less wealthy. But the lower classes suffered the most.

Within a short distance of the opulence of Mexico City's elite—sometimes just outside their windows—great masses of poor people lived in misery. More than 20,000 homeless people called *leperos* (meaning "lepers" in Spanish) roamed the streets begging.

Many of the poor people lived in *vecindades*. These buildings once were large homes for wealthy people but had fallen into disrepair. The Catholic Church bought the dilapidated properties, eventually becoming the largest landholder in Mexico City. The Church didn't make much money from the land, however, because so many poor people were unable to pay rent. Large families often lived in a single room. It was so crowded that people often slept crammed together on the floor. Sanitation and ventilation was poor, so diseases spread quickly.

In many Indian districts, people held on to some ancient traditions. Some Indians continued to worship the old gods in private. Annual battles between residents of different Indian districts reenacted ancient Aztec wars. The government tried to stop these war games by persuading the Indians to use stones, not guns.

A Divided City

Mexico continued to struggle under short-lived governments. The country even came under French rule between 1863 and 1867. Porfirio Díaz, a Mexican general who'd fought the French, brought political stability from 1876 to 1911. Although officially elected president for only part of that period, his power was that of a dictator. "Order and Progress" was his motto. He ruled Mexico with an iron hand, squashing any rebellions and lowering the crime rate. Under Díaz the city and the country modernized, and the wealthy accumulated more wealth.

Upper-class neighborhoods had street lights, multistoried office buildings, tram cars, modern plumbing, sewer systems, and opulent mansions. The elite copied European culture and sent their children overseas for schooling. A strong police force kept out the riffraff. Under Díaz wealthy neighborhoods were sealed off from darker-skinned people. Even the servants had light skin.

For the vast majority of Mexicans, life was very different. For them, economic progress and modernization meant low-paying factory jobs with 14- to 16-hour work days, often in unsafe conditions. The police kept things quiet in the wealthier areas but did little to fight crime against working people. In fact, poor people were afraid of the police, who would regularly rob them of money and even clothing. Those convicted of crimes were sent to squalid prisons. There were almost no hospitals and few doctors, drinking water was often tainted, and sanitation was poor. Some of the poor spent nights in flophouses, where people of all ages slept together in large rooms on straw mats. Those who did have permanent homes usually lived in shacks, with no running water, toilets, or sewers. Some of the poor neighborhoods were in such bad condition that civic leaders suggested burning them to the ground!

By the late 1800s, carriages had given way to trams, as wealthy pedestrians enjoyed a cool night in the Zócalo.

PIRATA
EL PIRATA
HIHUACAN

Large clay jars for water would be filled every day by aguadores.

Solid, ornate doorways became the hallmark of middle-class apartment buildings.

A Middle-Class Home, 1900

Under Díaz the middle class grew in size and importance. These people were neither rich landowners nor poor factory workers. They were shopowners, government bureaucrats, army officers, lawyers, engineers, and skilled craftspeople. Few were able to afford their own homes. Many lived in apartments that had been carved out of a former mansion. New doors were cut in the building so that every family could have a private entrance. The apartments had no toilets, but the inhabitants bathed in a public bathhouse, usually only once or twice a month (more often than middle-class people in Paris bathed at this time!).

Middle-class people often went out of their way to show the world they were doing well. Sometimes they used an entire month's wages on a single party thrown for friends. A great deal of money was spent on attending plays and musical entertainments. Many middle-class Mexicans hired servants even though they could not afford them. Servants of the middle class had to work hard for little pay. Although most of them had recently been poor, middle-class people often expressed great disdain toward low-income people.

Draining the City

Because of its location on a former lake bed, Mexico City was prone to flooding every time it rained heavily. This not only meant the destruction of property but also the spread of disease, since people had to slosh through stagnant water for weeks.

Throughout the site's history, many solutions had been tried. The Aztecs built extensive canals and dikes. In the early 1600s, Enrico Martínez, a talented engineer, had directed a massive drainage project. Some 60,000 Indian workers had labored for nearly a year to build a canal that was one of the great engineering feats of the age. But the canal was not maintained, and within 15 years it had become useless. The Great Flood of 1629 kept parts of the city submerged for five years! Many thought that Mexico City should be abandoned for another, drier site. Instead they repaired Martínez's canal and built other canals, tunnels, and dikes that he had recommended. The water slowly drained away.

By the late 1800s, Mexico City had grown seven times larger in size and in population, and Martínez's system was no longer big enough to handle the drainage problem. Every rainy season meant days or even weeks of boggy conditions. People walked with handkerchiefs over their noses to avoid breathing the foul smell that came from black ponds of water. Díaz was determined to drain the city for good. The $16-million project, which took 14 years to complete, was the largest construction project of his regime.

In 1900 the drainage system was dedicated with fireworks, cannon firings, ringing bells, and proud speeches. But only four months later, a flood again swamped the city, bringing traffic to a standstill. Several more floods followed in the same year. Díaz did not give up. The rivers were dredged. Although minor flooding still occasionally occurred, the major problem was solved at last.

Set in a bowl-shaped valley on a former lake bed, the site of Mexico City was prone to flooding, especially during the rainy months from June to September.

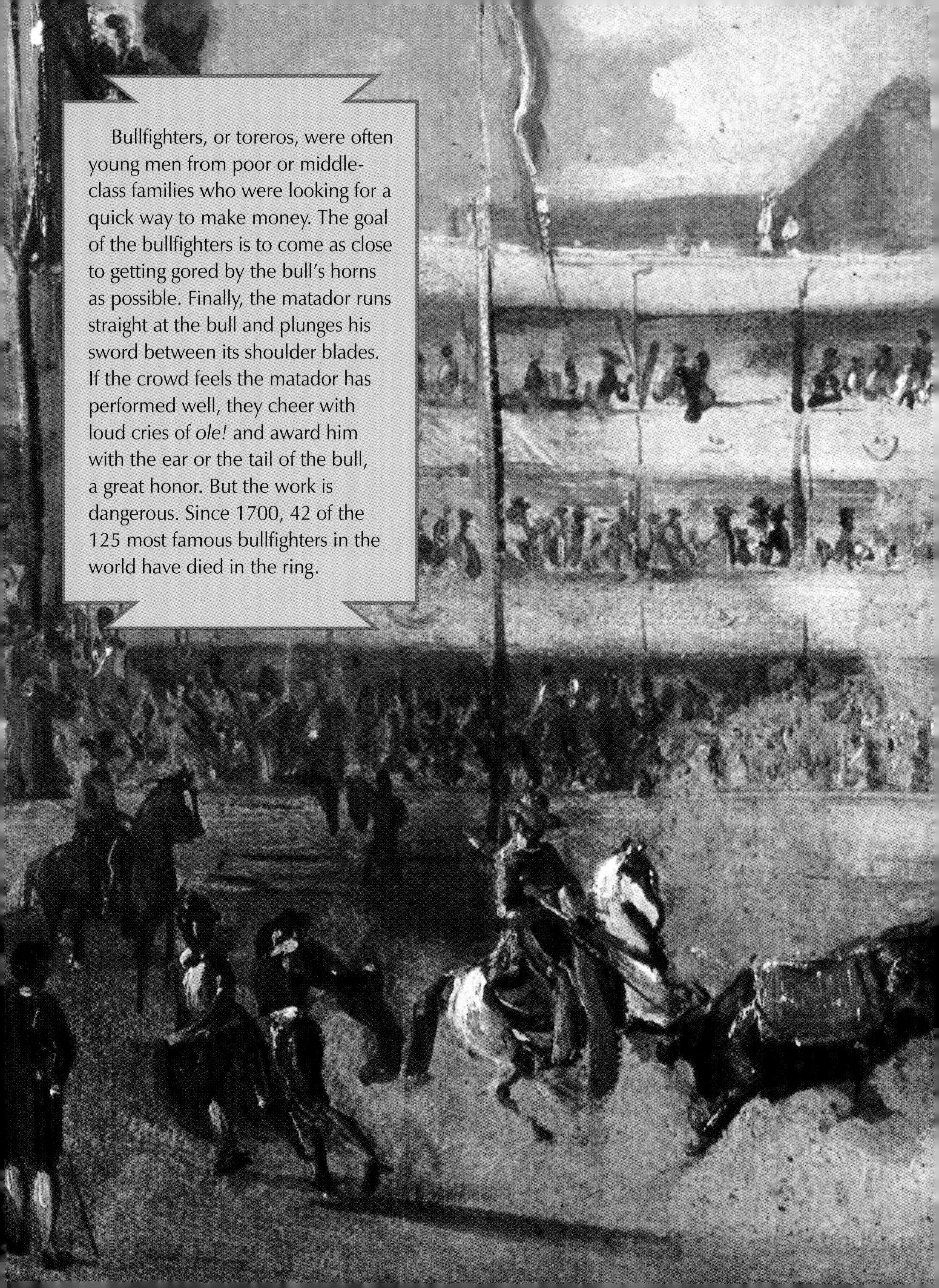

Bullfighters, or toreros, were often young men from poor or middle-class families who were looking for a quick way to make money. The goal of the bullfighters is to come as close to getting gored by the bull's horns as possible. Finally, the matador runs straight at the bull and plunges his sword between its shoulder blades. If the crowd feels the matador has performed well, they cheer with loud cries of *ole!* and award him with the ear or the tail of the bull, a great honor. But the work is dangerous. Since 1700, 42 of the 125 most famous bullfighters in the world have died in the ring.

Bullfight!

Bullfighting has been hugely popular in Mexico ever since the Spaniards introduced the sport. One seventeenth-century church official was such a fan that he had a private bullring built on the grounds of his palace. Bullfighting draws spectators of every economic level. But some Mexicans have labeled the sport barbaric and uncivilized. After one particularly bloody spectacle in which several horses were killed along with the bulls, some newspapers campaigned to abolish bullfighting. A law was passed outlawing the sport in the central district. But a new ring, well within the reach of city residents, was soon built to replace the old one. The Plaza de México in Mexico City is the world's largest bullfighting ring, seating about 50,000 spectators.

The matadors *(far left)* lure the bull with a *muleta* (a large red cloth). The picadors *(center)* ride into the ring on horses, force the bull to charge, and pierce him with lances as he runs toward them. A banderillero *(left)* uses a cape to lead the bull into making sharp turns designed to exhaust the animal.

Revolution!

In the countryside, workers on haciendas and in the mines grew more angry at their unhappy lot. Popular unrest against the Díaz government increased and erupted into a violent revolution. The Mexican Revolution (1910–1920) soon reached the capital, where various factions fought for control of the seat of power.

Fearful of military takeovers, Díaz had reduced the size of the Mexican army. Soldiers were mostly conscripts—men forced against their will to join and paid so poorly that they often deserted. Some deserters fought against the regime. The city became a battleground, especially during the Decena Tragica, the "Tragic Ten Days," of 1911. Rebels bombed or burned hundreds of buildings. Thousands of civilians were killed. Food was cut off,

Right: Díaz's soldiers about to attack an arsenal
Below: Zapata *(seated center)* and his men

and people starved or ate cats and dogs to survive.

After Díaz was overthrown in 1911, the various revolutionary factions fought for power. By 1914 four leaders had their own armies and their own ideas of how Mexico should be run. Emiliano Zapata wanted the land and wealth taken from the rich and given to the poor. Venustiano Carranza and Álvaro Obregón were less radical, wanting some reforms benefiting the poor but not wanting to overthrow the rich. Pancho Villa had no definite program except to steal from the rich and give to his army.

Chaos reigned as the Villistas and Zapatistas entered the city in 1914. Carranza and Obregón marched into the city in 1915 and established some order, but the city remained wracked by starvation. In the end, Obregón gained the presidency but enacted only modest reforms. The gap between rich and poor remained nearly as large as before.

Left: General Obregón's troops march into the city. *Top:* Pancho Villa's army *Above:* The city's defenses

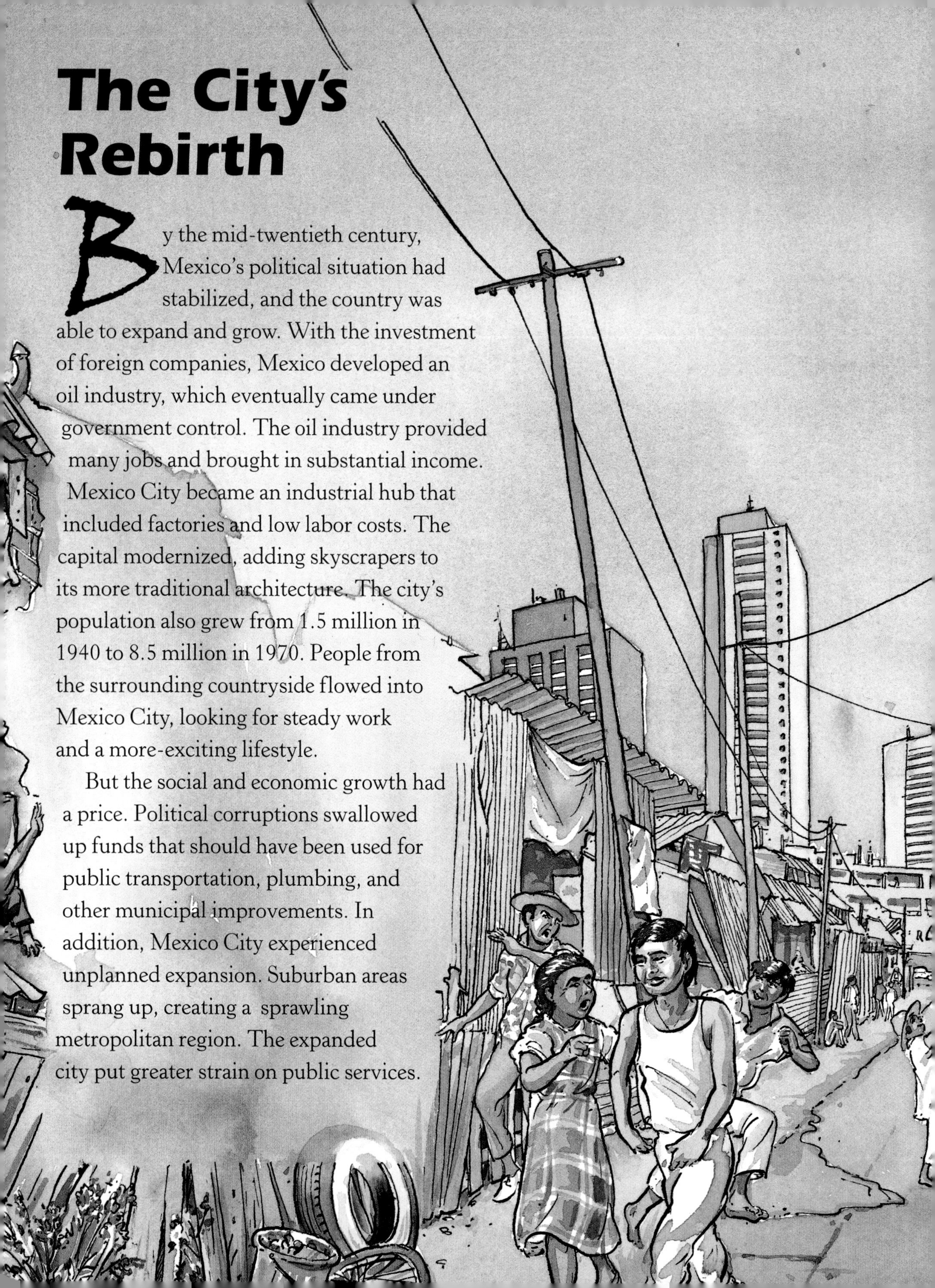

The City's Rebirth

By the mid-twentieth century, Mexico's political situation had stabilized, and the country was able to expand and grow. With the investment of foreign companies, Mexico developed an oil industry, which eventually came under government control. The oil industry provided many jobs and brought in substantial income. Mexico City became an industrial hub that included factories and low labor costs. The capital modernized, adding skyscrapers to its more traditional architecture. The city's population also grew from 1.5 million in 1940 to 8.5 million in 1970. People from the surrounding countryside flowed into Mexico City, looking for steady work and a more-exciting lifestyle.

But the social and economic growth had a price. Political corruptions swallowed up funds that should have been used for public transportation, plumbing, and other municipal improvements. In addition, Mexico City experienced unplanned expansion. Suburban areas sprang up, creating a sprawling metropolitan region. The expanded city put greater strain on public services.

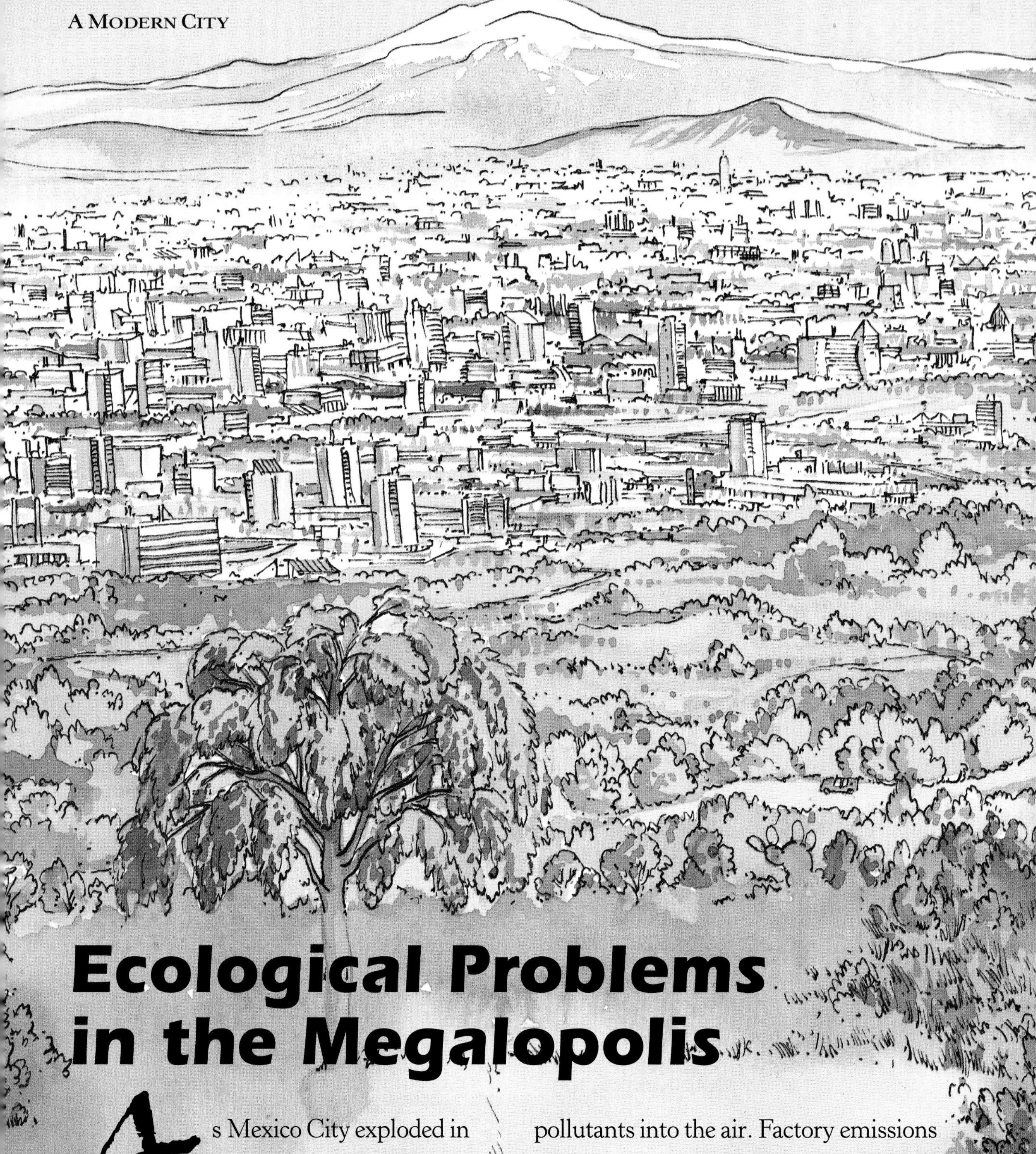

Ecological Problems in the Megalopolis

As Mexico City exploded in size and population—becoming a megalopolis, or immense city—pollution became a pressing concern. Millions of cars and trucks spewed pollutants into the air. Factory emissions added to the mix. The location of Mexico City worsened the problem. The surrounding mountains made Mexico City a sort of bowl from which pollution could

not escape. As a result, simply breathing the air became as unhealthy as smoking two packs of cigarettes a day!

City officials began taking steps to reduce the pollution. Cars and trucks have to pass strict emissions tests. Factories that pollute must cut down their emissions or move somewhere else. And mass transportation is being improved, so that fewer people will drive.

Mexico City, which once had too much water, is facing a serious water shortage. To meet the needs of an expanding population, the government plans to build canals and pipes that will bring water from a hundred miles away. But the plans are expensive and still won't be enough to supply all the city's needs. Residents will have to cut back, and factories will have to use water more efficiently.

Earthquake!

Mexico City sits on top of a fault, or place in the earth's surface where two tectonic plates meet. When the plates slide against one another, an earthquake results. Throughout the city's history, tremors and quakes have occurred from time to time. But one of the most destructive quakes took place on September 19, 1986. People living more than a thousand miles from Mexico City felt the upheaval. The capital's soft, spongy ground kept shaking after each tremor. Residents said it was like the buildings were sitting on a gigantic bowl of jelly.

The 1986 earthquake hit shortly after 7:00 A.M., when many people had just arrived at work or school. For three minutes, the city shook violently. Buildings crumbled and fell on pedestrians. Some people were trapped inside the structures. Thousands were buried alive. Telephones, electrical lines, radio, and television were quickly knocked out of commission, leaving people with no way of knowing what was happening in the rest of the city. Gas lines burst, and serious fires broke out. But no one could call the fire department. To make matters worse, government agencies that should have sprung into action moved slowly. Soldiers and police arrived, but they often just roped off the sites instead of searching for buried people. Official announcements tried to convince people that the disaster was not all that bad. But Mexico City residents knew better and came to their own rescue. Despite government warnings, citizens formed rescue crews to reach Mexicans trapped inside buildings.

In the weeks following the disaster, anger against the government grew. Many of the buildings that crumbled so easily had been built by the government and were supposed to have been strong enough to withstand earthquakes. In some cases, politicians had allowed shoddy construction to save money.

The earthquake awakened many Mexicans to the fact that they live in a precarious ecological situation. Not only must buildings be made safe from earthquakes, but the problems of increasing pollution and decreasing water supply must also be addressed.

Broken gas lines *(left)* led to fires. Across the city, people searched for survivors and valued possessions *(inset)*.

Hardworking Poor

In the 1970s, the oil industry was booming. But in the 1980s, the oil market changed. Too much oil was available, and prices fell quickly. Since then, Mexico has been in a financial crisis. Inflation runs high, and many people are unemployed. For these reasons, life for the low-income people of Mexico City has not gotten much better in recent years.

Many of the working poor live in large vecindades. The space is tight, and rooms are dark, but outside are patios where children play while parents chat. There is running water with which to wash clothes and to cook. Other neighborhoods, called shantytowns, are more grim. Often the people live in makeshift homes with no toilets or running water. Many of the adult residents have no jobs. Few of the children are able to go to school.

But even in the worst neighborhoods of Mexico City, people find ways to enjoy life. Local movie theaters and sports arenas provide cheap entertainment. Public transportation costs little, and government-subsidized stores offer food and other basic items at affordable prices. Festival days are celebrated with friends, and the streets are always bustling with activity.

Mural painting has had a long history in Mexico. The Aztecs painted large pictures on walls to tell their history. Spanish priests used murals to depict biblical stories. After the revolution, the new government employed artists to cover walls of public buildings with pictures that shamed the old rulers and promised a wonderful future.

Diego Rivera, a famous Mexican muralist, often celebrated the dignity of the poor. His murals have a strong political slant, depicting religious leaders and wealthy landowners as corrupt and revolutionary soldiers as heroes.

Rivera's painting, *Making Tortillas,* shows the everyday tasks of Mexico City's poor but employed people.

On the Day of the Dead, shops sell candy skeletons. Candles, marigolds (the Aztec flower of death), and photos of the departed decorate graves.
Wealthy countries have very few [holidays]: there is neither the time nor the desire for them, and they are not necessary. . . . But how could a poor Mexican live without the two or three annual fiestas that make up for his poverty and misery? Fiestas are our only luxury. —Octavio Paz

A City of Celebrations

The fiesta year begins on September 15 with El Grito Dolores, the preface to Mexico's Independence Day. On this day in 1810, Father Miguel Hidalgo y Costillo proclaimed Mexico's independence from Spain. Celebrations start when the president of Mexico appears on the balcony of the National Palace to repeat Father Hidalgo's historic proclamation. Then a replica of the bell that called Mexico to battle is rung. September 16, the official Independence Day, is dedicated to bullfights.

October 31 is the Dia de los Muertos, or Day of the Dead. During the festival, the spirits of dead relatives are said to visit the earth. The celebration begins when people meet in the cemeteries to bring toys, hot chocolate, and candy to the graves of departed children. Then people return home to sing, dance, and eat. The following evening, people go back to the cemetery, bringing gifts to loved ones. They pray until sunup, thankful for their fleeting reunion.

December 12 is the feast of the Virgin de Guadalupe, which attracts hundreds of pilgrims, many of whom crawl to a shrine in homage. In the chapel square, the costumed pilgrims take part in dancing and singing, often parading images of the Virgin. During Christmas festivities, celebrants knock on doors reenacting Mary and Joseph's search for an inn. Wealthy homes open their doors offering refreshments. Christmas gift-giving waits until January 6, the day of the three kings.

Street Vendors and Entertainers

Street vendors and performers have long been an important and respected part of life in Mexico City. For many people, selling on the street is a way to earn a decent living. Most vendors sell only one or two things, often something handmade. Following centuries-old traditions, street vendors whistle or sing short melodies that announce their wares. Rugs and serapes with bright-colored Indian designs are popular. Residents can find food at just about every corner—taco stalls, fruit stands, even floating restaurants in the canals. Sweet cakes, corn on the cob cooked over charcoal, and *jicama* (a cactuslike plant) covered with lemon juice and chile are some of the delicacies.

On busy streets, jugglers, clowns, and even organ-grinders with monkeys perform for whatever people choose to give them. Even poorer people are seldom stingy. If they like the show, they'll drop a centavo or two into the hat. *Tragafuegos*, fire-eaters, are usually teenaged boys who fill their mouths with gasoline and then blow it into a torch, producing a spurt of flame up to 12 feet long.

Of the musicians, the mariachi bands are the best known. Mariachi began as the music of revolutionaries in the countryside. The instruments—violins, guitars, and small accordions—were cheap and portable. Often a woman with a deep, husky voice did the singing. After coming to the city, mariachi bands kept some of the old trappings of rebel life. The performers wore eye patches, knives, and gun belts, just as the rebels did. More expensive instruments were added, especially horns and large stringed instruments. In modern Mexico City, mariachi bands are hired to perform at weddings and other celebrations.

Recovering the Past

At the National Museum of Anthropology in Mexico City, tourists and residents alike can look at relics from what has been called the Golden Age of Mexico's history. The museum includes not only artifacts from Mexico City's history but also has objects from all ancient Mexican peoples, including the Olmec and the Maya, who also developed impressive cities and social systems. The Olmec were artisans on a grand scale, producing carved stone heads that weighed many tons. The Maya are famous for creating one of the world's most accurate calendars. They had sophisticated systems of mathematics,

The carved stone yoke *(left)* is Aztec or Toltec, as is the crouching stone figure *(right)*. From Mexico City's colonial past is a ceremonial silver shield *(below)*.

astronomy, and language. They cut massive blocks of stone and transported them over long distances to build huge structures that have survived for more than 1,500 years. Their great cities were well organized and held many beautiful buildings. And they produced thousands of beautiful and powerful works of art.

Mexico City's long and impressive history is filled not only with times when a small, powerful group of rulers has taken advantage of most of the population but also with astounding accomplishments by everyday people. Too often, perhaps, the vast majority have been trapped toiling for long hours at low wages, with little hope of improving their lives. With democratic reforms and freer trade, Mexico City is poised to truly offer prosperity to all its residents.

Mexico City Timeline

1000 B.C.–A.D. 1502 Early History	**1000 B.C.**	Agricultural villages develop in Valley of Mexico
	A.D. 1175	Aztecs enter valley
	A.D. 1325	Founding of Teotihuacán
A.D. 1502–1521 Aztec Civilization	**A.D. 1502**	Motecuhzoma begins his reign
A.D. 1519–1822 Spanish Colonization and Independence	**A.D. 1519**	Hernán Cortés lands in Mexico
	A.D. 1520	Aztecs rebel against Spanish rule in the battle of La Noche Triste
	A.D. 1521	Spain conquers Aztec Empire
	A.D. 1629	Great Flood
	A.D. 1531	Juan Diego sees vision of Virgin Mary
	A.D. 1535	First Spanish governor
	A.D. 1600	Enrique Martínez begins his draining project
	A.D. 1692	Tumult of 1692
	A.D. 1810	Miguel Hidalgo y Costillo launches independence movement
	A.D. 1821	Mexican independence
	A.D. 1822	Agustín de Iturbide declares himself emperor of Mexico
A.D. 1864–1867 French Domination	**A.D. 1864**	French troops, sent by Napoleon III, invade Mexico
	A.D. 1867	Napoleon III withdraws troops

A.D. 1867–
Mexican Republic

A.D. 1867	Benito Juárez takes presidency
A.D. 1877	Porfirio Díaz becomes president
A.D. 1900	Dedication of Díaz's draining project
A.D. 1911	Beginning of Mexican Revolution
A.D. 1911	Tragic Ten Days
A.D. 1912	Liberal leader Francisco Madero becomes president
A.D. 1913	Madero's general, Victoriano Huerta, has him assassinated
A.D. 1914	U.S. troops seize Veracruz
A.D. 1914	Villistas and the Zapatistas take control of Mexico City
A.D. 1915	Carranza and Obregón march into Mexico City
A.D. 1917	The constitution is written, directed by Venustiano Carranza
A.D. 1920	Revolution ends
A.D. 1924	Mexican government limits power of Catholic Church
A.D. 1952	Benito Juárez International Airport opens
A.D. 1964	National Museum of Anthropology opens in Chapultepec Park
A.D. 1968	Summer Olympic Games held in Mexico City
A.D. 1970	Oil industry expands
A.D. 1980	Population of Mexico City reaches 15 million
A.D. 1986	Great Earthquake
A.D. 1990	Population of Mexico City reaches 22 million
A.D. 1992	Mexico signs NAFTA economic treaty with Canada and the United States

Books about Mexico and Mexico City

Baquedano, Elizabeth. *Aztec, Inca & Maya.* New York: Alfred A. Knopf, 1993.

Casagrande, Louis B. and Sylvia A. Johnson. *Focus on Mexico.* Minneapolis: Lerner Publications Company, 1986.

Coronado, Rosa. *Cooking the Mexican Way.* Minneapolis: Lerner Publications Company, 1986.

Davis, James E. and Sharryl Davis Hawke. *Mexico City.* Milwaukee: Raintree Publishers, 1990.

Fagan, Brian M. *The Aztecs.* New York: W. H. Freeman and Company, 1984.

Frost, Mary Pierce and Susan Keegan. *The Mexican Revolution.* San Diego: Lucent Books, 1997.

Goldstein, Ernest. *The Journey of Diego Rivera.* Minneapolis: Lerner Publications Company, 1996.

Kandell, Jonathan. *La Capital: the Biography of Mexico City.* New York: Random House, 1988.

Lilley, Stephen R. *The Conquest of Mexico.* San Diego: Lucent Books, 1997.

Marks, Richard Lee. *Cortes.* New York: Alfred A. Knopf, 1993.

Márquez, Herón. *Destination Veracruz.* Minneapolis: Lerner Publications Company, 1998.

The Mexican War of Independence. San Diego: Lucent Books, 1997.

Mexico in Pictures. Minneapolis: Lerner Publications Company, 1994.

Nicholson, Robert and Claire Watts. *The Aztecs.* New York: Chelsea Juniors, 1994.

Staub, Frank. *Children of the Sierra Madre.* Minneapolis: Carolrhoda Books, Inc., 1996.

Staub, Frank. *Children of the Yucatán.* Minneapolis: Carolrhoda Books, Inc., 1996.

Stein, R. Conrad. *Mexico City.* New York: Children's Press, 1996.

Stein, R. Conrad. *The Mexican Revolution: 1910–1920.* New York: New Discovery Books, 1994.

Streissguth, Tom. *Mexico.* Minneapolis: Carolrhoda Books, Inc., 1997.

Temko, Florence. *Traditional Crafts from Mexico and Central America.* Minneapolis: Lerner Publications Company, 1996.

Index

About the Author and Illustrator

Steve Cory is a writer and carpenter who lives with his wife and three children in Chicago, Illinois. Steve, who has a Ph.D in religion from the University of Chicago, has had a lifelong fascination with the everyday lives of ancient people.

Ray Webb of Woodstock, England, studied art and design at Birmingham Polytechnic in Birmingham, England. A specialist in historical and scientific subjects, his work has been published in Great Britain, the Netherlands, Germany, and the United States. He still finds time to teach young people interested in becoming illustrators.

Acknowledgments

For quoted material: p. 13, Miguel Leon-Portilla. *Aztec Thought and Culture: A Study of the Ancient Nahuatl Mind.* (Norman, OK: University of Oklahoma Press, 1963); p. 19, Leon-Portilla. *Aztec Thought and Culture;* p. 22, Bernal Díaz del Castillo. *The Discovery and Conquest of Mexico,* 1517–1521. (New York: Grove Press, 1956); p. 24, Toribio de Benavente Motolinía. *Memoriales: Libra de las cosas de la Nueva España y de los naturales de ella.* Second edition. (Mexico City: Universidad Nacional Autónoma de México, 1971); p. 34, Jonathan Kandell. *La Capital: The Biography of Mexico City.* (New York: Random House, 1988); p. 54, Octavio Paz. *The Labyrinth of Solitude.* (New York: Grove Press, 1985).
For photographs and art reproductions: North Wind Picture Archives, pp. 8-9; Bettmann, pp. 9 (three insets), 10-11, 44, 58, 59 (both); Stock Montage, pp. 12, 21, 36-37; EDI42188 118.798 Prisoners of War Sacrificed to the Sun God from an Aztec Codex (post-conquest, 1519). Bibliothèque Nationale, Paris, France/Bridgeman Art Library, London/New York, pp. 18-19; EDI142211 120.249 An Indian spy observes the arrival of a Spanish sailor on the Mexican coast, 1518 (manuscript) by Diego Duran (16th century). Historia De Las Indias. Biblioteca Nacional, Madrid, Spain/Bridgeman Art Library, London/New York, pp. 22-23; BAL4296 La Plaza Mayor, Mexico City, 17th century by Cristobal de Villalpando (1639–1714). Corsham Court, Wiltshire, UK/Bridgeman Art Library, London/New York, p. 25; BL22431 Mexico: Plaza Mayor de Mexico (print by Carl Nebel). British Library, London, UK/Bridgeman Art Library, London/New York, p. 30; Schalkwijk/Art Resource, NY, pp. 32-33; Art Resource, NY, pp. 40-41; Granger Collection, pp. 42-43; Corbis-Bettmann, p. 44; UPI/Corbis-Bettmann, pp. 44 (inset), 45 (left and top), 50 (inset); U.S. Army, Fort Bliss Museum, Fort Bliss, TX, p. 45 (bottom); Reuters/Corbis-Bettmann, p. 50; IND54394 131-0057630/1 Making Tortillas, 1926 by Diego Rivera (1886–1957). University of California, San Francisco, CA, USA/Bridgeman Art Library, London/New York, p. 53. Cover: Schalkwijk/Art Resource, NY.